Tell Us a Tale, Hans!

The Life of Hans Christian Andersen

By Dennis Brindell Fradin

Illustrated by Cynthia von Buhler

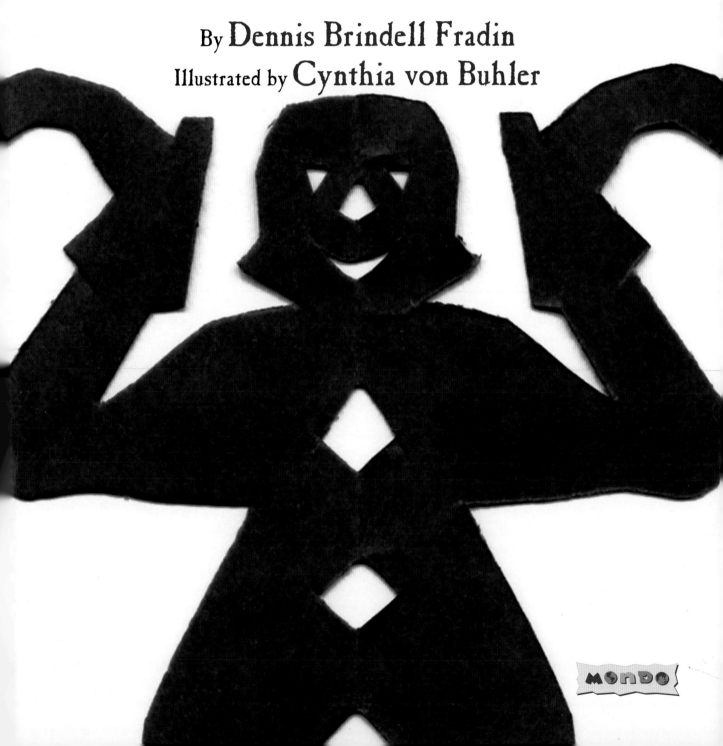

MONDO

An hour after midnight on April 2, 1805, a baby boy was born in a cottage in the poorest section of Odense, Denmark. His mother, Anne Marie Andersen, had been so poverty-stricken in her youth that she had begged for coins in the streets. The infant's father, Hans Andersen, was a shoemaker with few customers. The child was named for his father, with a middle name added.

And so he was christened Hans Christian Andersen.

Odense was located on one of the hundreds of islands that belonged to Denmark. A lovely coast, numerous lakes, farms, windmills, and castles helped make Denmark one of the world's prettiest little kingdoms.

Denmark's people, called the Danes, were known for their love of books. Even poor shoemaker Andersen spent much of his meager income on books. During Hans Christian's first days on Earth, his father read comic plays aloud to him. But instead of laughing, "I kept screaming at the top of my voice," Hans Christian later explained in his autobiography.

It was fortunate that Hans Christian was an only child, for his tiny home on Munkemolle Straede (Monkmill Street) had no space for anyone else. The single room was jammed with his father's shoemaker's bench, a table and chairs, a bed, and a crib. As a young child, Hans did not realize that his family was poor. He thought that every child lived in a crowded cottage and occasionally went to sleep hungry. In fact, he later recalled his childhood as filled with little joys.

On the walls, his parents had pasted pictures, perhaps obtained from calendars or from their church. Hans Christian would stare at the pictures until the far-off places and biblical scenes almost seemed to come to life.

Stories were the boy's greatest pleasure. Before bedtime his father read to him from a big book called *The Arabian Nights*. Although she had never learned to read, his mother would tell him old tales she had heard. She told him about Odin, the ancient one-eyed Norse god who ruled the Universe. Odin had founded Odense and had given the town his name, Anne Marie claimed. During thunderstorms, Odin's eight-legged horse could still be heard galloping across the countryside.

5

Scattered around Denmark were boulders that giant glaciers had left behind long ago. According to Anne Marie, the boulders had been thrown across the water and onto Denmark by witches. Up in church steeples lived elves with red caps who helped kind people, his mother continued. She told Hans to be wary of the spirits who lured children away from their homes with their beautiful songs.

Sometimes his mother took Hans Christian to the town's home for poor women, where she had some old friends. While they worked at their spinning wheels, the old women told him stories about trolls, ghosts, and mermaids.

When Hans Christian was six, a glowing object with a long tail appeared in the night sky. The Andersens went to St. Knud's churchyard to look at the strange object. Anne Marie and some other onlookers feared that it was a sign from heaven that the world was ending. Nonsense, declared Hans Christian's father. It was just a comet—a natural body orbiting the Sun. Hans Christian was relieved that his mother's warnings of doom turned out to be wrong. The stories his mother and her friends told weren't necessarily true, he now realized, but he enjoyed them nonetheless.

At about the time of the comet, Hans Christian's father bought tickets and took his wife and son to see a play at the Odense playhouse. Hans Christian was enchanted by the actors, the theater, and the audience. Since his family could rarely afford to attend the theater, the boy did the next best thing—he helped put up posters advertising the plays. He was allowed to keep a poster from each play as a reward. Hans Christian would stare at his posters for hours and imagine he was at the plays.

Seeing that his son loved stories and plays, the shoemaker built a miniature wooden theater and puppets for him. Hans Christian learned to sew by watching his father make shoes. He obtained scraps of cloth and thread from his parents and sewed costumes for his puppets. He loved to sit with his puppet theater and make up tales about princes and princesses, mermaids, witches, and haunted castles.

"Bravo!" his parents would yell when he performed his puppet plays for them. Sometimes he accompanied his mother to the stream on washday. Then he would stand on the rocks and sing and dance for the women who gathered to wash clothes. "Bravo, Hans Christian!" they would call out. Hearing the applause, Hans Christian knew what he wanted to do when he grew up. He would write plays—or become a singer—or a dancer—or an actor.

By the age of seven, Hans Christian had started school. But instead of doing his lessons, he sat daydreaming about stories he was composing for his puppet theater. One day as his mind wandered, the teacher hit him with her rod. Hans Christian ran home to tell his parents, who sent him to another school. The tall, thin boy with long yellow hair continued to daydream while he was supposed to be learning to read and write, but his classmates liked him. They gathered around him in the schoolyard to hear him tell stories.

Meanwhile, Denmark had gone to war. In those days rich men could pay poorer men to take their places in the army. Thinking that the army would be his road to wealth, the shoemaker accepted a rich man's offer to take his place as a soldier. Hans Christian missed his father, who was gone for a year and a half. He finally returned in 1814, still poor, and ill as well. Before his death in 1816, he told Anne Marie his wishes for Hans Christian: "No matter what the boy wants to be, even if it is the silliest thing in the world, let him have his own way."

After her husband's death, Anne Marie became so poor that she had to wash other people's laundry to earn a living. Hans Christian could no longer attend school. He needed to work to help support his mother and himself. So Hans was sent to work in a cloth factory, where at first he helped the men run the looms. But when they discovered that Hans Christian could sing and tell stories, his fellow workers offered to do his job while he entertained them. One factory worker was jealous of Hans Christian, however. He poked fun at his long yellow hair, said that he sang like a girl, and pushed him. Hans Christian ran home and told his mother, who never sent him back to the factory.

In 1818 Anne Marie married another shoemaker. Hans Christian was now 13—time for him to think about his life's work. Since he was skilled at sewing costumes, his mother wanted him to become a tailor. But Hans Christian still dreamed of becoming a writer, a singer, an actor, or a dancer. When he was just 14, he asked his mother if he could go to Denmark's capital, Copenhagen, to seek fame and fortune.

At first his mother refused to let him go because he was so young. However, recalling her husband's dying wish for his son, she finally relented. Besides, she believed he would be scared by the big city and would soon return home.

On a September day in 1819, Hans Christian walked to the city gate of Odense with his clothes in a bundle, a loaf of bread, and several coins in his pockets. He tearfully kissed his mother goodbye, then off he went in a horse-drawn coach. Because Copenhagen was an island city like Odense, he had to make the hundred-mile journey partly by carriage and partly by ship.

To save money, he hadn't paid the full fare to Copenhagen. Therefore, after two days of travel, he was let out of the coach near Frederiksberg Castle, the summer residence of Denmark's King Frederik VI. After exploring the castle gardens, Hans Christian walked the last ten miles to the Danish capital.

He had never seen such a place. Copenhagen had 120,000 people—fifteen times the population of Odense. People were everywhere—wealthy people zipping along in fine carriages, street vendors selling everything from fish to newspapers, and beggars wearing rags.

Hans Christian found a place to live in a storeroom—a single room with no lights or windows. But with few coins remaining, he couldn't afford anything better.

Hans Christian decided to seek work as a dancer. His second day in the city, he dressed in a suit that he had outgrown and a hat that was too big for his head and walked to the home of Anna Margrethe Schall, the Copenhagen Ballet's leading dancer. A maidservant who answered the door took one look at him and tossed him a coin.

"How can you think I came to beg?" he indignantly asked the maid. He wanted to dance for Madame Schall, he explained, so that she would help him get a job with the ballet.

The maid led him inside, where Madame Schall agreed to watch him dance. Hans Christian took off his boots. Pretending that his hat was a tambourine, he danced a scene from the play *Cinderella* in his stockings. Madame Schall watched in amazement as the youth with thin legs, big feet, a long nose, and yellow hair leaped about her parlor. Once he finished, Madame Schall showed him to the door, saying that he had no future as a dancer but could stop by for an occasional meal.

Although disappointed, he remained hopeful that one of his other talents would help him find a job. At home, he had often been praised for acting all the parts in his puppet shows. Within a day or two of visiting Madame Schall, he went to see Count Holstein, the manager of Copenhagen's Royal Theatre. Count Holstein wouldn't even let him try out for an acting part. Looking Hans Christian up and down, he pronounced "You are too thin for the theater."

Hans Christian was deeply wounded, yet still convinced that he would find a place in "the world of beauty," as he called the arts.

Back home in Odense, Hans Christian had won praise for his singing voice. So one day, he visited the home of Giuseppe Siboni, director of the Copenhagen Academy of Music. He barged in while the famous musician was giving a dinner party. Nonetheless, Hans Christian was led into the drawing room and invited to sing for the gathering of musicians and writers. When he finished singing, everyone applauded. Siboni offered him free singing lessons.

This didn't change the fact that Hans Christian was still poor. However, in Copenhagen it was the custom to invite needy people to supper one day a week. Hans Christian found several people he had known in Odense, and through them made many new friends. Among all these people, Hans Christian was invited to supper nearly every day of the week, so at least he was able to eat.

Still, by the time his first winter in Copenhagen arrived, he had holes in his boots, and his clothes were in tatters. Someone gave him a blue topcoat to protect him against the cold. But since it was several sizes too large, Hans Christian stuffed it with newspapers, giving him a resemblance to a scarecrow. To make things worse, he caught a bad cold. Soon he was so hoarse that he could barely talk, let alone sing. Months passed without his voice improving. In the spring of 1820, around the time of Hans Christian's fifteenth birthday, Siboni told him that he had no future as a singer. "Go back to Odense and learn a trade!" his voice teacher advised.

Instead of going home, he renewed his efforts to become a dancer or actor. He spent so much time backstage at theaters that he was finally given minor parts in plays and ballets. When visiting or writing to his mother, he exaggerated his achievements to make her proud. He was on the stage, headed for fame, he told her. Actually, if not for the generosity of friends, he might have starved.

When he was about 16, Hans Christian decided that since he had always loved making up stories, he was meant to be a writer. The problem was, he had daydreamed through his brief schooling and could barely read and write. So, at the age of 17 he entered a school where his classmates were roughly half his age. He attended school for nearly five years. Although he still wasn't much of a student, he finally had learned to read and write.

Next, he wondered, what kind of author should he become?

Hans Christian tried many different kinds of writing. He wrote plays. Some theaters even performed them, but the plays were not very memorable. He wrote a poetry book, but poetry experts didn't like it. He tried writing novels, but he never became a great novelist. One book he wrote actually sold *no* copies and was chopped up and sold as wrapping paper.

Now and then, just for fun, Hans Christian would write what he called "wonder stories" for children. Much like the stories he had made up long ago for his puppet theater, they were about princesses and mermaids, witches and haunted castles. Some were based on old tales he had heard from his mother and her friends in Odense. Others came out of his head, inspired by his own experiences. In 1835, not long after his mother died, his first wonder stories were published in a pamphlet.

At first these stories received little attention. Hans Christian Andersen himself considered them less important than his writing for adults and never expected them to amount to much.

He was wrong. Word spread among children—and their parents—that the stories were wonderful. They became so popular that each year at Christmastime, a new volume of Andersen stories would appear. Many of the nearly 200 tales he wrote became children's classics. One, "The Ugly Duckling," is about a baby duck who can't find his place in the world. Another, "The Little Match Girl," is about a poor child who sees magical visions on a freezing night. Other famous Hans Christian Andersen stories include "The Little Mermaid," "The Emperor's New Clothes," "Thumbelina," and "The Snow Queen." By the age of 40, Hans Christian Andersen had become famous for his wonder stories, which people today call fairy tales.

In his later years, Hans Christian Andersen was hailed as one of the world's great authors. He wrote *The Fairy Tale of My Life*, a book that describes his long struggle to find his place in the world. He traveled to many lands and was introduced to kings and queens. And wherever he went, children gathered around him and said, "Tell us a tale, Hans!"

Author's Note

I heard my first Hans Christian Andersen tales as a child when my teacher read us "The Emperor's New Clothes," "The Ugly Duckling," and "The Little Match Girl." I loved the stories without wondering about their author. Only when I came across Hans Christian Andersen while researching another subject a couple of years ago did I become curious about his life. The result is this book.

Much of the dialogue and information in this book came from three of the numerous versions of Hans Christian Andersen's autobiographies: *The Fairy Tale of My Life* (British Book Centre, 1954), a book by the same name by Paddington Press, 1975, and *The Mermaid Man* (Library Publishers, 1955). Also helpful were *Hans Christian Andersen* by Jackie Wullschlager (Knopf, 2001), *Hans Christian Andersen* by Fredrik Book (University of Oklahoma, 1962), *The Wild Swan* by Monica Stirling (Harcourt, 1965), and *Hans Christian Andersen,* edited by Svend Dahl and H.G. Topsoe-Jensen and published in Copenhagen in 1955. —D.B.F.

For my granddaughter, Anna Rose Fradin —D. F.

For Cody, Shane, Julian, Louie,
and my parents, Frances and Louis Carrozza —C. v B.

For information contact:
MONDO Publishing
980 Avenue of the Americas
New York, NY 10018
Visit our website at www.mondopub.com

Printed in China
07 08 09 10 11 12   HC   9 8 7 6 5 4 3 2 1
09 10 11 12   PB   9 8 7 6 5 4 3 2

ISBN 1-59336-681-7 (HC)   ISBN 1-59336-682-5 (PBK)

Designed by E. Friedman

Library of Congress Cataloging-in-Publication Data

Fradin, Dennis B.
   Tell us a tale, Hans! : the life of Hans Christian Andersen / by
Dennis Brindell Fradin ; illustrated by Cynthia von Buhler.
      p. cm.
   ISBN 1-59336-681-7 (hardcover) -- ISBN 1-59336-682-5 (pbk.)
   1. Andersen, H. C. (Hans Christian), 1805-1875--Juvenile literature.
   2. Authors, Danish--19th century--Biography--Juvenile literature.
   I. Buhler, Cynthia von. II. Title.
PT8119.F69 2006
839.8'136--dc22
   [B]
                                                                    20050167